LA⌷

⌷ ⌷⌷

MEDICINE

INTRODUCTION

Here is your own personal pocket compendium of laffirmations— quotes by our masters of mirth to help you transcend troubles and gain power over pain—hopefully without milk coming out of your nose. Sure, laughter's the prescription for a whole bunch of modern-day ills, from isolation to stress, but more than that ... it's fun!

With wit and wisdom from an all-star cast of wise humorists and visionaries—from Charlie Chaplin to Alan Alda, and from Erma Bombeck to Wayne Dyer—this little treasury inspires you to tap into the power of laughter. Lighten up, laugh out loud, hold hands and jump, reach out with a smile, heal thyself, and remember that the playful life is the life worth living. After all, as Oscar Wilde wrote, "Life is too important to be taken seriously."

A DAY WITHOUT LAUGHTER IS A DAY WASTED.

CHARLIE CHAPLIN

It is impossible for you to be angry and laugh at the same time. Anger and laughter are mutually exclusive and you have the power to choose either.

WAYNE DYER

A good laugh
and a long sleep
are the best
cures in the
doctor's book.

IRISH PROVERB

Laughter is America's most important export.

WALT DISNEY

Mirth is God's medicine.
Everybody ought to
bathe in it.

HENRY WARD BEECHER

WHAT SOAP IS
TO THE BODY,
LAUGHTER IS TO
THE SOUL.

YIDDISH PROVERB

The more you
find out about
the world, the more
opportunities
there are to
laugh at it.

BILL NYE

I was irrevocably betrothed
to laughter, the sound of
which has always seemed
to me to be the most
civilized music in the world.

PETER USTINOV

You don't stop laughing because you grow old. You grow old because you stop laughing.

MICHAEL PRITCHARD

Laughter is
inner jogging.

NORMAN COUSINS

When people are
laughing, they're
generally not killing
one another.

ALAN ALDA

Laughter and tears
are both responses to
frustration and exhaustion.
I myself prefer to laugh,
since there is less cleaning
up to do afterward.

KURT VONNEGUT

A CLOWN MAY BE THE FIRST IN THE KINGDOM OF HEAVEN, IF HE OR SHE HAS HELPED LESSEN THE SADNESS OF HUMAN LIFE.

RABBI BAROKA

Laughter is the shortest distance between two people.

VICTOR BORGE

You cannot hold back
a good laugh
any more than you can
the tide. Both are forces
of nature.

WILLIAM ROTSLER

To make mistakes
is human; to stumble
is commonplace;
to be able to laugh
at yourself is maturity.

WILLIAM ARTHUR WARD

Always laugh
when you can.
It is cheap
medicine.

LORD BYRON

You can't
stay mad at
somebody who
makes you
laugh.

JAY LENO

A good laugh
is sunshine
in a house.

WILLIAM MAKEPEACE THACKERAY

THE IMPORTANCE OF LAUGHTER IN MANAGING YOUR BUSINESS RELATIONSHIPS IS OFTEN NEGLECTED.

MITCH THROWER

If you can't
laugh at it,
you're taking it
too seriously.

NATHANIEL SUMMERS

Laughter is
the language
of the soul.

PABLO NERUDA

Anything that gets you
to release the stress
in your life and really
laugh is worthwhile.
It can heal the planet.
It truly can, and
it actually has.

LUCIE ARNAZ

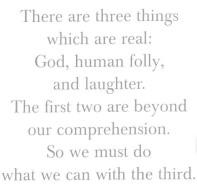

There are three things
which are real:
God, human folly,
and laughter.
The first two are beyond
our comprehension.
So we must do
what we can with the third.

JOHN F. KENNEDY

The person who
knows how to laugh
at himself will never
cease to be amused.

SHIRLEY MacLAINE

You can turn painful situations around through laughter. If you can find humor in anything—even poverty—you can survive it.

BILL COSBY

IF YOU CAN'T MAKE IT BETTER, YOU CAN LAUGH AT IT.

ERMA BOMBECK

Laugh and the world laughs with you. Snore and you sleep alone.

ANTHONY BURGESS

The person who can bring the spirit of laughter into a room is indeed blessed.

BENNETT CERF

Laughter is
an instant
vacation.

MILTON BERLE

Let me play the fool.
With mirth and laughter
let old wrinkles come.

WILLIAM SHAKESPEARE,
The Merchant of Venice

One should take
good care not to
grow too wise
for so great a
pleasure of life
as laughter.

JOSEPH ADDISON

You grow up on
the day you have
your first real
laugh at yourself.

ETHEL BARRYMORE

NOBODY EVER DIED OF LAUGHTER.

SIR MAX BEERBOHM

The difference between an optimist and a pessimist? An optimist laughs to forget, but a pessimist forgets to laugh.

TOM BODETT

If we couldn't laugh, we would all go insane.

JIMMY BUFFETT

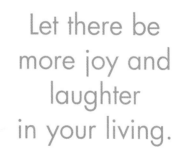

Let there be
more joy and
laughter
in your living.

EILEEN CADDY

Laughter is
the tonic,
the relief,
the surcease
for pain.

CHARLIE CHAPLIN

The earth
laughs in
flowers.

E. E. CUMMINGS

Laughter is
a tranquilizer
with no side
effects.

ARNOLD H. GLASOW

LIFE IS TOO IMPORTANT TO BE TAKEN SERIOUSLY.

OSCAR WILDE

Laughter is
the most healthful
exertion.

CHRISTOPH WILHELM HUFELAND

Dad always thought
laughter was
the best medicine,
which I guess is why
several of us died of
tuberculosis.

JACK HANDY

He laughs best who laughs last.

SIR JOHN VANBRUGH

Laughter is the
sun that drives
winter from the
human face.

VICTOR HUGO

You're never
fully dressed
without a smile.

MARTIN CHARNIN

Laughter is by
definition healthy.

DORIS LESSING

Nobody really cares if you're miserable, so you might as well be happy.

CYNTHIA NELMS

'Tis a good thing
to laugh at any rate;
and if a straw can
tickle a man,
it is an instrument
of happiness.

JOHN DRYDEN

At the height of
laughter, the universe
is flung into a
kaleidoscope of
new possibilities.

JEAN HOUSTON

Laughter is the sensation
of feeling good all over
and showing it principally
in one place.

JOSH BILLINGS

You can't deny laughter; when it comes, it plops down in your favorite chair and stays as long as it wants.

STEPHEN KING

A laugh is a smile
that bursts.

MARY H. WALDRIP

A MAN ISN'T POOR IF HE CAN STILL LAUGH.

RAYMOND HITCHCOCK

Smile—sunshine
is good for
your teeth.

AUTHOR UNKNOWN

Laughter is
the best way
to make
somebody's
heart beat.

ROBERT HOLDEN

He who laughs, lasts.

MARY PETTIBONE POOLE